INTER ALIA

DAVID SEYMOUR

INTER ALIA

Brick Books

Library and Archives Canada Cataloguing in Publication

Seymour, David, 1971–
    Inter alia / David Seymour.

Poems.
ISBN 1-894078-45-4

I. Title.

PS8637.E95I58 2005   C811'.6   C2005-903458-0

We acknowledge the support of the Canada Council for the
Arts, the Government of Canada through the Book Publishing
Industry Development Program (BPIDP), and the Ontario Arts
Council for their support of our publishing program.

The cover photograph is by the author.

The book is set in FF DIN and Minion.

Design and layout by Alan Siu.

Printed by Sunville Printco Inc.

Brick Books
431 Boler Road, Box 20081
London, Ontario N6K 4G6

www.brickbooks.ca

30 Years Young

Brick Books 1975–2005

This book is for my parents, Ron and Garie Seymour.

The words are for my wife, Karen.

Contents

Nomenclature of the Semi-Precious

Inter Alia

Occasionally we still have the feeling that violence has long been done to the thingly element of things and that thought has played a part in this violence, for which reason people disavow thought instead of taking pains to make it more thoughtful.

—Martin Heidegger

Anyone whom the little man looks at pays no attention; not to himself and not to the little man. In consternation he stands before a pile of debris.

—Walter Benjamin

Nomenclature of the Semi-Precious

you have to go, already you can feel you're
somewhere else, deposited,
you're washed up in some other life as
insubstantial as a stone.

—Don McKay

Amber

The hugeness of the fact of them. They look
extraterrestrial, salt- and bone-coloured skin,
sharing inaudible ageless gossip, one foot
planted firmly in the grave. The oldest are unswayable,
even with that fat westerly huffing off the Pacific.
So remote, they no longer understand
ground: where you and the insects eke out days.
Light sieves through the upper boughs,
tip-toes over the younger needles. The air
under them is a murky syrup, some turbid
afterthought of nature. Forget the blisters
and cracks of history, unstirred memory, lost love.
These are the real McCoys, the hard copies. Pious.
Fossils of regret. A mosquito lands cautiously,
with a dim fear, the need to tap coursing blood.

Peridot

You are difficult and disappointed
on the long drive home from the party:
love can be citric, even stern when you let it.
Waves break into the harbour, slush noisily
against the sand. The moon is a burnt
photograph. I try not to think of turtles
nosing into traffic, their blind faith in light,
or worse, of tires pulling toward the deeper water—
green and magnetic—in our silence. We pass a farmhouse,
then an orchard, but the apples can't be seen.
They pitch and bob in the humid air;
bruising one another gently in the darkness.

Black Opal

A blip, a nothing on the x-ray
of things. But it occupies space
with the opacity of a cataracted eye.
As though wet light has landed
then slipped away finding a deeper gravity,
its absence excessive. Dark stones trapped
in the walls of a grave have to be dislodged
before the coffin can be lowered and lie
properly. That must be someone's job.
The doctor is returning
with an irrevocable diagnosis.

Heliotrope (Bloodstone)

—for Phaethon

Inconstant bastard child, it's not news
you weren't the favourite before, but this
takes the cake. One of the horses
smashed its foreleg and is off to the factory;
your dad won't hear the end of it for months.
A bright flash of light, they said, like the sun
landed in the backyard, then all hell broke loose.
At first, they thought the sound was
the thump and thunder of the white horses
careening into the barns and the old man's house.
Like a shooting star in the daytime, they said.
Some joyride. Scorched body rolling on the waves,
petals of blood blooming in the dark water, face turned
in a smile toward the breaking clouds.

True Chalcedony

Waxy, dull dreams, their patient tug
through the stillness, then sleep is over.
The blankets feel waterlogged, eyes sting
in the flat light. A storm's been rolling in all morning,
clouds belly-full but no rain yet. Dense threshold.
Outside, a cavity to be filled with names,
details. Burnt toast and the eggs are too hard-boiled,
you can't mistake that inner leaden gleam.
Each day is more porous, coming and going
as if it were someone else's. Any minute now,
wonder what on earth you're going to do.

Lapis Lazuli

Russia, Afghanistan, America, Chile. Bad tourist,
don't quite fit in and never want to visit
the attractions. Not cold, afraid of desire.
Unpracticed. At night, the hotel employees
make love wildly by the ocean, then fall asleep.
The tide douses their small drift-fires, deposits
souvenirs from the sea. Spending each
afternoon indoors close to the window,
counting the shells, *damn this heat should've broken,*
dreaming you were a sliver of sky.

Quartz

To the east, a carpet of fiddleheads
unfolding and unfolding into the boreal
yellow dusk. Deep south, there is a heat
the branch of each nerve learns
to anticipate. Somnolent and towering
Saskatchewan cloudheads repeat for miles.
North: snowflakes shake off
the frost-bitten atmosphere;
their fractal stammer into being.
                              Beneath us, the earth
keeps a record, performs mathematical feats,
proving various collisions inhabit
unmoving objects. Shy entropy,
shifting from clarity to cold clarity.
Each compact, tangled clew unravelled
by the threadbare, shot-through light.

Topaz

—for T.T.

There is no mystery, but the answers
have all been wrong. Here crescendos fail.
The muteness of heavy snowfall and a chestnut-
brown warmth hide the smaller lives drifting
quietly from view. Only fingerprints remain,
a circle of breath on the window, and the uneven
temperament of nightfall. Dust in the vent is burning.
The man downstairs who plays the Spanish guitar,
he is weeping again. How many times
can the same story be told?
We are not the earth's.

Almandine

How susceptible this instrument, the body. Humming
through the bones as we drift into sleep, catacombed
music like a deep, confused narcosis: we've listened
in the wrong direction our whole lives—the stars
are unimportant. With no extra vibrato,
no arpeggio, the voices translate us,
chart voluptuous graphs on our skin,
and receive the dead, singing.
The heart, at rest, understands
one sound, one colour.

Moonstone

A black-and-white classic glides across the screen,
but the sound is turned down, so I'm left
with questions about plot and the radiant,
near-blue flicker filling the living room. Wisps of smoke
hover on the lips of some sexy dame in a ball gown. Perfect
cleavage. On the other side of town, under tonight's
full harvest white, the drive-in has finished its double bill.
The cars with fogged windshields are the last to crunch
out of the lot. In the valley, coyotes are dining
on the more curious neighbourhood cats. This late,
though, everything wears a halo. Time for the close-up.
Whatever she's saying now looks tart and polished,
but the anger is lost in the softened lens.
Lady, I'm going to miss you when you're gone.
When we're all gone.

Tourmaline

Past the finger-thick roots
of oak, clarity almost unappealing;
a lack of blindness in the dark. A taper.
Immaculate fitness of colours
waiting under the earth
like a hidden season. Know: true
silence is necessary to love.

Inter Alia

When one complains about the meanness of Others, one forgets this other and even more frightening meanness— namely, the meanness of things were there no Other.

—Gilles Deleuze

Photograph of an Old Room

The blackness, the whiteness
exclude the sun and yet
the vase of tulips, the window,
the salt and pepper shakers, remain lucent,
cling to their own light.

Everything is not being what it was.
The two tables try to keep up appearances
while the mahogany cabinet seems clumsy in
the bounded silence. Even the gimcracks
on the mantelpiece aren't quite gimcracking,
their intimate insignificance glossed over
by one dustless, untouchable surface.

Something palpable, but something
more than solidity, is absent,
replaced by embarrassment, or fear.
Imagine: leaving a well-lit, favourite place
getting home to bed and realizing
you'd forgotten your body there: imagine
running from the single mercy
in an otherwise indifferent day.

What is left is the beautiful,
bewildered sadness of human things
sensed briefly
on the edge of the visible,
hidden by use and affection.
Look, the objects stand glistening.

Early Morning City

A low menace of clouds, a muffle.
The room we enter
when we sleep, its colony of empty seats,
the long corridors into the world, everything
gone missing.
                    I shift in bed
when the light falls,
like wet snow, on my shoulders
and my hair—
something has been torn,
a wound in the air, in the heart
a silence. The sky
congeals to a bruise.

All the cats in the city
are padding through the alleys
into other, paler darknesses.
And the stones of the old buildings
begin to grow into their grey,
quietest and most alive.

Injured Swan, High Park

Your stillness is a disturbance,
cyclists and joggers stop to take a look.
A boy wades into the pond and lifts you out of the reeds.
His sister places almonds, bites of apple
on your wide back, rushes to their father in a fit of giggles
then gathers the courage to return and stroke your feathers.
You tolerate it all patiently, steadying the pain
with a casual grooming, careful not to brush
against your unfurled left wing.

If everything were made of light
you would still have arrived first
and arranged yourself in the middle of things.
The whiteness of your body bends the afternoon around it,
like a childhood fever; airy cotton sheets,
cold facecloth, glass of water on the bedstand,
the whole room weightless, unfastened from its colours.
                              Like drifting, sourceless music
that tells the rest of us we are only half-formed,

accidental. I wait for you to raise your looped neck,
voice your disapproval and burst out over the water,
because, no, you shouldn't be here among us,
except that your broken wing
has made you heavier than air,
heavier, now, than ever.

Rain Dance

Because of the heat the people
crowd on the corner
        to watch the brawl, become
bloodhounds in the bristling
close-the-oven-door afternoon,
know nothing but the weather
that steeps inside them,
                buttering their skin
and the inflamed faces of the two
middle-aged men.

They stand apart
ham-handed, circle in
drowsy curtsies
        and slow jive
trade clumsy swings, jab
the air sluggishly
        and bob
and weave, heels dragging,
shoulders hunched in search
of the target and the one blow,
a reservoir of strength to dislodge
the last piece of ice
folded deep in the other's brain.

They circle for maybe ten minutes,
                sway under
the weight of the sun like drowned bodies,
the thick clot of air an invisible ocean
rolling between two heart attacks:
lung-shaped stains
sweating through their shirts,
waves rising off the softened tar
                and dodge

and feint, muscles slack with fatigue,
blocked traffic leans on horns.
There's a fevered yell for blood
or a downpour;
                    the crowd begins to mutter,
                    turn their backs.

Then with reclaimed urgency,
not blooming from anger, but drought
        and release, a punch breaks through
the swelter, whistles
        past that almost elegant
slow-motion violence:
                            the fist's
        fluency in air and
                bone embracing resistance.

In autumn

when the air is animal, loping off

in search of other dens, when the light

keeps its hands to itself and your laughter

is honed on the day's blade,

I understand the sharp

dark edge of things, the trapped

clarity left behind on your face;

how summer's fat body can lean so quietly

away from us.

Perlerorneq

— a Killinemiut word which, roughly translated, means
to feel the weight of life in winter

It is time to save the things
I might otherwise have thrown away,
leaves eddying around the trees
colour frozen in the vein, scarf of sparrows
winding through the empty branches.
At evening the sunlight strikes the houses sideways
like thinning blood. Children and shadows
quickly vacate the neighbourhood.
There is a point when animals,
badly confused, or simply
tired of homing, do not return but go
farther astray, like memory, farther north—Igloolik,
Tromsø, Komolomec—become cold bones forgotten
under drift; winter's resolution. But I will grow
a fur of transparent hairs to collect
leftover light, a pot belly for warmth, I will
practice reading in the dark, develop
a leanness of vision, clean past contour.
I will wander outdoors measuring each footstep.
Steadily the Arctic hares burrow into twenty-two
hours of nightfall, caribou taste the air;
they know wakefulness differently, know places
where no one wants anyone to be.

Lines for Elora Gorge

I am thirsty, you are pure water
I am weary, you are energy.
—traditional Turkish poem

that the river troubles and courses, frothing the backs of stones
whose weight is hunched shoulders, drowned purpose, *carry me*
whose weight does not recognize us
that pale and deep-green lichen find purchase in the cliff-face
that the heat is an open mouth
                    the cedars redden and moisten
that the lilacs form soundless judgements, swell space
                    while the wind waits at closed doors
that the swift shaves the water once with its breastfeathers
that the day is disarmed and uncertain
                    the light is brilliant, builds nothing
that night will spill into the gorge
and empty the limestone's precipitous eyes
that they bear no trace of envy
that the heart, so thick and falling, reels
that the blue airless blood will climb

Ten Day Poem for Saskatchewan

Winter wheat under a full moon;
who owns that paling face
in the window?

The New Year falls on Monday.
I watch an old woman
walk backwards into the wind.

Ahead in the lane
a monk patches the crossroads
with sod from the garden.

Empty late-day fields,
vesper bells toll
in the rain.

Saskatchewan fields:
the wind makes mountains for crows,
tumbling backwards and down.

With a doubled heart
I approach the cooped hens,
the slim-netted light.

Why do I feel lonesome?
Ah! The cows' breath smells
like a Maritime wind.

If I had wings
I'd be another crow
to the owls in the aspen.

Only a light breeze,
the cows scratch their necks
against the barbwire fence.

Clouds passing northeast
their shadows scud over the field.
I hear the trees bending.

I go to sleep
with the lady's-slippers you saw,
and the scrawny fox.

Shooting hoops:
off the rim—too many words
swish—good haiku.

Heart before head:
the tick saves his one jump—
waits for you to pass.

Head before heart:
the tick barely hangs on
to the deer's rump.

Travelling to Danceland:

> On the horsehair dancefloor
> prairie women two-step
> in flat-heeled shoes.

Travelling to Quill Lake:

> Watching shorebirds
> the scent of sage opens
> under our heavy feet.

A polite bow from the cattail.
Its yellow head,
the call of the blackbird.

The snow geese will arrive,
blanket these summer tracks
before winter.

She sketches your shoulders.
The gulls and white pelicans
float over the world.

Kyōka

The man shined his car all day.

The man, having shined his car all day,
has developed a natural, circular rhythm.

93 Eagle Talon Esi—4.3L V6 Vortec, 5spd., pw, pdl, ps, cc, tilt, p-moon,
approx. 125K hwy, 40K on rblt eng. 97, blk bty, blk. lthr int., blk. ext. 1
yr. or 20K fact. warr., exc. cond., clean in/out, must be seen.

The language can run on empty,
though it purrs like a kitten,
the language is loss roughly handled.

The man, having shined his car all day,
can see his face in the hood.
                              Our bodies
are not-large-enough mirrors.

The man, having shined his car all day,
thinks he might take it for a spin around the block.

There is a site in the brain
where the linguistic articulation of a thought
prior to speech is believed to occur.
It is Broca's Area.

Thought, it says, *thought, come over here*
I want to show you something.

I think I might take the car
for a spin downtown, the man says to himself.

Broca was a man who now claims
part of your brain. The pink
slips. Broca didn't even have a license.

Drive through the centre of a metropolitan city.
Inhale the wreckage. Breathe out.
Everything is beautiful from a distance.

The man, having shined his car all day,
has developed an appetite.

Construe construct contrapt:

                              radiation commotion
                              emergency shower
                              absolute surveillance
                              utile storage
                              olfactory warehouse
                              automatic harmony:

                              hog barn 100,000 sq. ft.

the leftovers are in the refrigerator.

Once the language thaws
the engine will start.

The French translation
for the Anglicized Japanese word *Kamikaze*
is *le Chinois fou.*

Everybody loves foreign cars;
they're more reliable and have higher top speeds.

The man, having shined his car all day,
having taken his car for a spin,
having stopped on the way at the drive-thru,
now parks it carefully in the shed
to protect it from the rain.

He built the shed last year,
out of pine,
with his own two hands.

The Cat Forgets

The cat forgets the sandpaper
shush shush of tongue
against paw
before he preens his whiskers. Using

the crook of the paw for a tongue.
Like trying to write a voice,
or music—

the face of the mind
   washed clean,
smiling at the effort.

The Organ of Corti

I

Hearing too is often forgotten.
Sounds are forged in the small,
complicated accident
of inner ear.

It begins with a rhythmic strum and bones
the size of fleas,
fluttering hind legs
as they bite
        the brain.

Primitive but reliable.
Workers and collectors
esoteric as the dinosaur jaw, the age of fossils.

Sounds take shape
when the hammer strikes
the anvil, unearths an ironwork of

stirrups, catching
the foot noiselessly in midair.
Hearing is a fox hunt
with the pomp of opera:

voices and instruments passing
through the anvil chorus,
permanently.

II

Clank, grumble, stir.

Relying on the hammer, anvil, stirrup
alone
    related,
relaying electric stampedes
                down
the spine
where staggering academies of thought turn
solid,
    range across our systems;
open-mouthed, toe tapping,
heart chugging up the throat,
sotto voce for Bach?
            With laughter?
Finger snap,
      the hand's interminable gestures.

III

Sounds reveal sounds. Avalanche, earthquake
found by the slim tremor in a wavelength.
Cellos lie across anvils, strings down.
Inside the tenor's
throat, a hammer blow, the ear
swells, the bones
        strain,
the music of your body begins.

Red Panties on the Windowsill

Tricky toss. Some woman's performed a strip-tease
off the penthouse balcony of the hotel
and managed to leave me a souvenir.
When I dumped my bags and threw open
the thick polyester drapes my first view of Mexico
(*oceanfront and inground pool with waterfall bar*)
was not the bottom-heavy sky, a blood orange
plunging into the Pacific, or even the overheated,
disinterested horses asleep on the beach. No, instead
a migrant cardinal dead from fatigue, feathers still ruffling,
wait ... that's no animal, must be a child's spent piñata
a dozen roses are roses are—these blushing
castaways, travelling on the wind from god
knows what height to land here; lost,
embarrassed tourist on the sill.

Back home they were awkward, unmentionables
set to dry on a backyard line with hubbie's
black socks and chinos, the calamity of numerous
indelicate wedgies: calving the suburban glacier
of some plump, untanned ass from Missouri.
Now, out in the world, they've become an intimate
telegram, *in flagrante delicto*. The kind
of silk and lace that's been pranced in,
ogled, shimmied to ankles. Feeling foreign,
a little afraid of their new predicament. Trying
to involve themselves. I'm sure I hear a mariachi band
begin a flamenco in the streets.

Two Brass Candlesticks

Gift, paperweight, bookend, ashtray,
window prop. They dwell in each use

the way memory dwells on distance. Once,
in the hands of a drunken friend

they entered a conversation,
two urgent and bold exclamations.

Having lived so many lives they are now
unsure of themselves, quietly holding lavender candles.

Their slenderness belies a density that is
weaponlike. A heavy love for fire.

Late at night, when my back is turned;
Remember, she said, *when you light these.*

Inter Alia

There are no secrets among the objects, and they do not love.
Rabbit-punching the senses: carousels, sneakers
dangling off telephone wires, perfumes
lost on the air, all of the city's empty arenas;
and hair on a barbershop floor, rain
past the wooden doorframe, wet grass,
vacant rocking chairs on the porches;
stoic, unmoving. Plotting wild escapes
from the human world.

Somewhere there is an engine
whose thousand parts are running flawlessly.

At home: an apothecary filled with cures
for loneliness. The worn furniture, the books, the appliances,
each usable item defends its grace. Even the television
investigates other landscapes, setting distant views
in motion. How many things that were gifts
can you count in this room? The phenomena
commiserate by remaining indifferent and desirable.
Confront them, stare them down and they tighten their grip.
Native. Planetary. Restless. They cannot even sleepwalk
into life. There were once favourites with stories—
lucky coins, photographs. Clothes comfortable as nudity.
We are growing old, less passionate
for unnecessary details. If only.

A Word on Silence

You the word won by silence.
—Paul Celan

because silence is an open window in the house

because silence is the third party, a strategy
                    for hunted birds (and they must nest also)

because silence is called after, because silence
                    is sometimes asked for and ceases to be, because

silence is a great lip-reader, adlib-er, and shrewd con artist
          and the way we try to think like hills,
                                        which is probably wrong
because not even poplar leaves say so little

because those cumulonimbus are not alone in their aloneness

because silence is the life prairies lead,
                              a touchstone,
          a rib cage of ideas bringing mettle to the bone,
          the discarded shell

because silence is the listening ear of each word

because silence can't decide on a reply

because silence, this is ground control—we are ready for liftoff

because silence is before we begin. Let me explain.

There is a violin in its case and the bow is waiting

because silence is one more colour
                    which makes the heart sink

because silence stencils haiku on the wind, and try as we may …

it is the eye of the eye watching coyotes
                    linger on the edge of town,
and an unspoken question will remain

because silence makes me feel that you are attending

it is alone in this world, I see it on the streets
          begging for currency

making the most of bad jokes by laughing

because silence dicks around and maybe the animals are right

because silence is,
                    bridging nights, disregarding days

smells like boreal forests
            after rain, tastes
like a coin from an old woman's purse,

because it looks like what I want

because silence basks in the sun and settles on the dust
                    on the sweat on the skin
                            covering my bones

because silence is a lick,
                    a lyric in your ear

a lost friend, the drunk in the ditch, the plough-horse
            put to pasture

because silence is the beaver's diligence and the dam's
                    incorruptible patience with water,
the lips of lovers before the hand caresses,

because silence is the shadow of what is difficult
            is the still power of beauty

it strips language and leaves it standing like a naked man
            in a crowd who still insists he has secrets to keep. No,

because silence romances everything, reasonably,

knows the earth was born too early for us latecomers

remains unfit to struggle with us

because silence is that August night,
            the night that hangs lowly, when each sound
            becomes clear but furtive, cautious as prayer.

The night that traps vestigial light
beneath a coal-black body as it stuffs
itself with trees and heat,
a covered hump crippling dusk
and the friendliness of strangers
under its dark gravity, because the night
is an elephant that refuses to listen,
rise up and rumble on its way,
a raven's final bluff, perfect poker face.
Because the night is heaven's edge
scuffed raw by gravestones, a yawn for the dead,
a gasp from the moon's perfect mouth, such luminous skin
and muscle; because tonight knew it would discover
the heart's interior, enter those unlit rooms
and whisper, *the time that steals your days*
is not death, but the space to remember.

because silence is what I remembered during the day

                                                                    then laughter
                        the rest was a rude noise

because the precise nature of truth will be unforgettable and speechless

            as we design ever more eloquent prisons: each spoken word

because silence is alar, and in the absence of a body or cargo
                        beats its wings unsuccessfully

                                    is disabled by rivers and streams, and cannot
            sunder the ice in winter

because silence haunts us like the phantom pain of amputees

because all of those who have died, and are certain, are unavailable
    for comment

because the most sophisticated surveillance equipment involves three
            bones and a drum

because whoa black betty blambalam, and brass sections,
and because Bach was born
with fingers

because you can cram fistfuls of it into Dizzy's cheeks

because silence tells me what I have said falls short

because silence is golden

because I heard a noise earlier, and stood up, and peered out

it hovers in the lungs on the inhaled breath

because after silence is not my voice but the dimmed hum of the world

because pelicans have nothing left to say when they reach adulthood

because silence is eventual

because I came into this world screaming and will not go gently,
but cursing and annoyed, and doubtful

because it is a gift and a wound,
because

silence is a wild-kicking jig, it is, it is,

it is so

Head Arrangements:
Twelve-String Poems for Huddie Ledbetter

The Sinful Songs

Rhymes with Judy, not muddy. A man named Huddie Ledbetter was born January 1888 in Caddo Lake, Louisiana near Shreveport. Huddie grew up quickly beside his father in the cotton fields: a six-string at fourteen, horse at fifteen, six-shooter at sixteen. He's a good knocker, good with his fists, and woos the girls on the dance floor. Another man named Walter Boyd was born on the lam in De Kalb, Texas, 1917. Quiet fellow, likes the women, day-labours for the local landowners, breaks the pride of the nastiest broncos. Can put a bullet in the head of a family member at twenty yards. Another man named Lead Belly was born in the camps of the Sugarland pen, 1920. Has metal in his guts but a voice so blustery it blows him right over the prison gates. Always has the luck of the devil. All three play the twelve-string like kings among ordinary men, find freedom in that mahogany and spruce. Laughter and tears. Children understand this immediately.

All I want in this creation is a little bitty wife and a big plantation.

A sound on the wind wakes him, so he sneaks past Australia's pallet to the open window and peers out. The darkness around the log cabin is skin-tight, but for the odd flare of a burning stump the oxen can't root from the earth. Even the stars are gone. His mamma and papa are still somewhere in the fields clearing brush with uncle Terrell. Further off, as his eyes adjust, the low north sky brightens with the halo of a bonfire: a sukey jump at old Simms' farm. The oily smell of roasted peanuts and rabbit fat blows in gusts from that larger, fainter light. Holding the windjammer Terrell brought from Mooringsport, he strains for snatches of music above the mild din and echo, trying to mimic the melodies; faster than the church spirituals. The buttons aren't placed conveniently for a seven-year-old's fingers. Australia lies awake listening now, but doesn't say a word as her brother plays. One by one, the stump fires wink out. This gift from his uncle, all he owns.

I laid down last night, turnin' from side to side, I wasn't sleepin'—I was just dissatisfied.

This isn't his first trip to Shreveport, but his mother seems more adamant, distrustful of the place. Nineteen miles is a fair trot with a guitar on his back, he shrugs the fretted neck from his shoulder and hums to himself for nerves. When he was six, ten years gone now, his father drove him, wide-eyed, down Fannin. Cotton bales as large as buggies lined up in the middle of the street. They were piled high on the sidewalks, too. Stray tufts wafted in the air, an unending snowfall trying to out-season the leaden humidity. It stuck to derbies, bared shoulders, the sweating horses. Later, waiting for papa, a brilliant and confusing red-lit night beneath that white drift, barrelhouse pianos belting out from the saloons, shadows of women in the upper windows. Slowly, he sifts his fingers through the loose sugar in his pocket, stolen from his mother's pantry. In case he gets beer tonight for playing. Much as he's tried he can't abide the bitter taste. Money's always better.

Ada got a gold mine, Ada got a gold mine, Ada got a gold mine way above her knee.

He uses his voice as a beacon while Lemon stumbles, reaches for the sound, stumbles again, then with a sudden clear instinct heaves his great bulk onto the steps of the car as it retreats from the Dallas platform. Inside, the conductor sees their instruments and doesn't bother asking for tickets. By the next stop they've fangled a new ballad for the passengers. Their rendition of *Fare Thee Well, Titanic* begins to loosen purses. Lemon smiles—squint-eyed cherub face on the body of a grizzly—as quarters plink into the tin cup. He can tell when it's a nickel or a dime. During a break they sip whiskey, talk about their wives, Lemon just nineteen and newly wed, wrestling, bootlegging. The train slips past Silver City, Waxahachie. Watching his friend ride the neck of the half-empty bottle along his guitar strings, listening to the coiled steel twinge and complain. Like an old salvaged feeling. Dark as this starless night, those icy waters of the North Atlantic.

I'm sitting here wondering, would a matchbox hold my clothes.

Loud and powerful as a well-made woman. An easy rider. Stella, the auditorium model. His first is painted green as a young cornfield, and so big the slightest touch sends a raw wow and shudder through the hollow belly. Mahogany back and sides from Honduras, German spruce top plate, American birch fret-board, rosewood bridges and inlay. Mixed pedigree; twice the size of Blind Lemon's Hawaiian. He buys it in Dallas second-hand for ten dollars; two thousand pounds of picked cotton. The action on the twelve, heavy-gauge steel strings is loose but difficult, the kind of jangle his ropy forearms have wanted to dance with for years. There is an avoided violence, a perfect artlessness in the chords—bass octaves running off with the croon in his voice. Or, the poise of an arranged idea, as though he's heard this sound in his head all along and just needed to find its proper instrument. Outside, while he plays, the world's forest fires burn with abandon.

If yo' house catch afire an' dey ain' no water roun', throw yo' jelly out de window, let de doggone shack burn down.

They could paint his mood with the darkness in the sky. Not too many men take that much joinin' about a woman. It's funny, they don't actually hear the shot, but live inside it. A hammer clicks and the whole world pauses, except Ellic, already far into the forest before you can smell the powder scorching the mild December air. Then there's the sound of a hickory switch tearing skin, and the argument ends like a casual conversation. Will Stafford just stops talking and falls. Just like that. Dies in his new white tennis shoes—they all bought a pair for tonight's party. Ellic and Lee are long gone. He looks down at his cousin, a black hole in his forehead, the quiet gape of his mouth a final insult, and knows he's going to miss the dance. The ground begins to hurtle. Tears are rolling down his face, though he has no idea. From the Texas banks he can see Oklahoma, and freedom, across the dry Red riverbed. No water this time of year, so close to Christmas.

I've been to the river, and I've been baptized. Now take me to my hanging ground.

So many birds chatter in the forest, he can barely make out the barking. Thirty years; five months served. His breath comes like the fast, bright burn of a knife in the ribs, but he struggles through to a second wind. The stale sweat on his prison-stripes is candy to them; leg irons their dinner bell. At evening, he sinks into some rushes on Bend Lake. The moon floats by above the bristling treetops. Two homesick mockingbirds. Then a voice startles him awake—*Get on out of there, Walter, or I'll shoot your black heart out.* Empty promises. He turns away deliberately and wades deep enough to taste the tepid water. Thirty years. A hound lunges in and he grips it tightly, drags it under the surface as the others bellow, blood-mad on the leash. The trackers finally beat and haul him thrashing to the shore. They won't even let him drown. The moon has disappeared into the trees. More than anything he misses a woman's fingers on his back while he plays.

Where did you sleep last night? In the pines, in the pines, where the sun don't ever shine.

Five past eleven: the metallic, intermittent whistles from Houston mark out time in the darkness of the cell. A few minutes later the South Pacific's lights begin to scream and flicker across the ceiling, unstrung film clacking on the reel. He watches with feigned disinterest. So close. Today it felt like the sun's clock stopped as it hung in the middle of the sky. Two new boys dropped dead in the fields, despite the steady belt of his voice leading the line, keeping the pace workable. Fear makes them swing harder, faster than he hollers. Cotton, corn, and cane; somewhere, people being clothed, fed, sweetened up quite nicely. He listens to the men murmur names of lovers and wives in their muscle-bound sleep. The passing train-light paints each face with a look of tense concentration. Roberta, Julie Ann, Silvy, Irene. Another line comes to mind and he reaches for the pencil and pad hidden under his mat. Almost finished. Governor Neff arrives in a week.

Shine its light on me; let the Midnight Special shine an ever-lovin' light on me.

At least he's drunk enough not to feel any pain. Even manages to sing while the doctor threads the needle through his abdomen. *Eight surface lacerations circling the stomach from kidney to kidney, no muscle penetrated.* Martha, pretty as ever, met him at the door this morning with a razor in her hand, tired of excuses. He closes his eyes, more wounds to add to the map across his body: head laid open by a whiskey bottle during a fight, an ocean of blood, his fingers left numb for years. Neck parting like the Red Sea mid-song onstage in Oil City, someone's jealous boyfriend cutting the music short. And early in his teens: a seam from the corner of his left eye down his cheek, slender flick of a switch-blade tracing a riverbed for tears. The doctor is finished, so he reaches for his guitar to play a few for the nurses. So much anger and revenge, charted out with scars. And now this belt of forty stitches from his wife: an archipelago.

Wednesday we were sittin' down talkin', Thursday she pawned all of my clothes.

He refuses to leave the kitchen to play for the Albany College professors gathered in her parents' parlour. Sits down with the giant guitar on his knee and undoes his bowtie, absentmindedly running two fingers along the scar that cuts a valley across his neck. *I'm going to stay with you, Miss Kate.* She is delighted and terrified. She's never seen hair so white, like fresh snow; bright as the gas-lamp. He sings well past bedtime (the adults have long forgotten them), tries to teach her the Buzzard Lope, the Eagle Rock: shaking one foot in the air, flapping his featherless arms toward an awkward landing against the table, rattling the used dinner crystal. Unforgettable bird. His voice softens the later it gets. Katie laughs and tries to hide her yawns, she wants to glide like this, on the toes of his polished patent shoes, the whole night. Her friends will just die. Between the dance lessons and his quieter songs, the gin from the pantry cupboard is slowly disappearing.

I'm dreaming tonight, of an old southern town, the best friend I ever had.

Martha touches the back of his neck with her fingers and tells him it's time for dinner. He's been at the kitchen table all day tuning and untuning, playing songs half-speed, as though listening for answers in the silence between the chords. $18 for his performance at the Workers' Alliance meeting last night; it keeps the pot full. Woody, Brownie and Burl are on their way over. Each will bring a bottle, of course: the unspoken entrance fee. Martha's cooked for everyone, but the two of them eat before the others arrive. Later, when the guitars and voices really start to rail, the kids down the hall sneak in fresh-faced among the adults' legs. Finding a place to sit becomes a balancing act, even the bed's full. And then Sara Ogan begins, her voice so thin from the TB they have to mute their strings to hear it. An unsteady whisper. The whole room leans in. This crowded lower East Side tenement, a keel in the New York night. Lungfuls of waiting air.

We're in the same boat, brother. And if you shake one end, you're going to rock the other.

The loss is fathomless. His mind the one window left unbroken, watching the body leave ahead of its time, a towering disconnectedness. Unable to conceive of the inability to fingerpick the last note, toe-tap, undo a shirt button: the unflawed senses sensing the gradual lockdown, jar in the jaw, keyless throated slurs, voice a grey goose flown, lungs floating in doldrum under his weatherless unfed muscle, the spine's messages stutter shyly, lost alarms, limbs asleep and dreaming, hands in their final terminus at his sides, the door can no longer be opened. He begins to live outside his own story. They don't play records or the radio in the corridors of Bellevue Ward R6, though Martha's asked. Not many visitors allowed either, and those that do come don't know what to say. He stares at the flowers, condolence cards. Stella's in the room, too. Hasn't been tuned in months. Now that he can only listen, does it matter whether he hates or loves this silence?

The last time I seen him, he was flying 'cross the ocean, lord, lord, lord.

Inter Alios

We look almost happy out in the sun, while we bleed to death from wounds we know nothing about.

—Tomas Tranströmer

The astronauts are waking up

above us, their dreams cross
the sky. Floating out of bed
they drink orange juice from the air,
tune in stray sports broadcasts,
are lonesome for gravity.
Canseco fans, fans, steps back from the plate
and the transmission frays.
They put on silver suits, secure
their helmets and, unafraid of the vacuous cold,
drift off the satellite. Good morning, stars.
The Earth is a flung curveball, sunlit
at the seam. It casts a mountain
shadow on the aviators. They laugh
with one another in different languages.
What can possibly be, is,
only larger, weightless and unconcerned.

Waiting While You Sleep

I listen to music that sounds quiet and dusty,
like old photographs. No rain tonight.
If there were, it would have torn
the glass from our windows, turned time over,
thrown distances on its small shoulders,
words in their right order.

Light webbed in the boulevard trees, a bike
stolen while I watched, the cat left the house—
his belly brought him back.
Then meteors.

The camera was heavy, I shifted and lost the picture.

As green as jade but milder
like wafting feathers, like conversation
like waiting; easy really, something
the wind and weather won't change,
as casual as crossing an empty road,
your body's the gold
of streetlamps.

Six Meditations on Breasts

So many: not edges but curves:
touching the throats of sparrows.

Just your breasts, rising then sinking
in sleep—and now I can't.

What defiance; steaming after a shower,
the apples sulk in the kitchen.

Buttons, clasps, hooks: how gingerly
the strap slips to your elbow.

These days are thin, but wine
and fresh-baked loaves of bread.

For you, love, a ritual; I give
these hands, their fumbling ceremony.

I could rouse her

but now she is

beneath the apparatus,

a body in full weep,

a music so attuned to living it cannot be heard:

it would be a sad thing to mean

nothing when we sleep

The Plain Fact of the Matter

Holding the cup in your hands, white. Watching it find a way
to your lips; the time it takes a cigarette to reach my mouth.
You look as though you are about to expose yourself, give
up some secret. Or not. Your finger circles the rim which
catches your gaze; the one thing this moment you want
to understand without words. Ever have. Right before
I speak, you cock your head, bring your ear in close
for this new, less cruel language—in the cup, the
shy turn of your neck.

Smoke is exhaled, broomswept dust in a sunlit room.

Promise

Chunky black velvet boots, salt-stained,
down jacket and midnight-blue jeans, every morning
I watch her step onto the bus and break the safe,
populated silence—imagine she walks up
the aisle to a soundtrack, finds a seat, leans her head
against the window, and listens. *You're pre-occupied*
with Fridays, want a better job, remain uncommitted
to any struggle, and have not begun to die, bleached
blonde hair, red scrunchy flecked with silver,
nicotine for perfume, chewing gum nervously,
you might have more lovers this week than I've eaten
eggs, are worried about becoming a mother too soon.
Probably has two brothers, no sister. I realize
I'm staring and turn briefly to the window. *Where*
do you go; delivering yourself daily
from your memories with promises? Chipped
fleshy-peach nail polish, eyeshadow the colour
of fresh bruises. Doesn't have a watch. *You live*
a series of secrets, like the rest of us,
but wear them openly, unafraid. If I could
whisper something more than the weather in her ear
as I move to the door, touch her hand, a strand of hair
accidentally, a question might be answered
for the both of us, the city could change its ways,
confirm the existence of ghosts. *My eating habits*
trouble me, I would say, *this winter has been long,*
I have a knapsack of overdue books to return
to the library. She won't hear this as another song.

Words Are Rain in the Womb of a Cloud

Language is an indiscretion.
Language is telling, it locates
your voice in the storm's centre.

The glimmer in your eyes
let me know
this was not a conversation
but the vertigo of high plateaus,
being caught naked at a window,
the drapery flung wide,
                                billowing.
That stare struck me dumb.

Was it possibly fear of lightning? Possibly,
the delicacy of your wrists,
when they moved as you spoke,
                        unnerved me.

Utility (*A love poem for Jeremy Bentham*)

Performance aside, the mechanism alone should require voluminous
manuals, several years apprenticeship. Yet it's more difficult to get a driver's
licence. The technique of manufacture, while often criticised as too highly
sophisticated, is beyond reproach, demanding little in the way of upkeep
and supported by built-in redundancies, resiliency effects. Asymmetrical
design compromises neither stability nor balance. Utile functions continue
perfunctorily, even while operating under the influence, or when confronted
with severe behavioural stress:

so why then,

in the middle of my workday,

does this muscle, this ticking
engine the heart, ka-chunk and flex
the brain, make memories tense
their long lean backs,
and remember you momentarily?

Ghost of a Chance

A mother and her daughter stop in front of a shop window.
The mother points at the display and smiles in an effort to
cheer the girl up. The girl, glowering, looks up and for the first
time in her life sees not her mother but a woman whose name
she doesn't know. The mother tightens the collar of her jacket;
how that stare from her daughter terrifies her, how something
as lost as love can still be vicious and unforgiving.

What is it that gives us over like this? When speaking
becomes too intimate and painful, and listening slows down
until each word crawls to some halting, unforeseen recognition
of one another. The girl forgets the episode as it happens. Her
mother has grown perceptibly older by the time they reach
home.

There are no borders between us—a windless, moonless
silence. The house you were raised in gets torn down. A ten-
year-old letter, left unopened. News of a death in the family. We
can turn away from loss but not toward anything less difficult.
People hurry along the sidewalks after work. They gutter like
flames in the cool air, desiring other places. To linger into the
evening, into the rare light that can wake you from a day-long
torpor, and watch them leaving for home. To do only that.

More Accidents
after C.D.

Adam bruised his eye and received
a hairline laceration across the forehead,
sustaining five unreturnable jabs and a left hook.
Laura stabbed her palate with a dessert fork.
The pie, unfortunately, was delicious.
Drunk, bereft of words, Mark
fell asleep and rolled onto the campfire.
William's foreskin separated while dry-
humping Patty on the first date.
Sandra turned to look when Sarah shouted duck.
Though the motorcycle was a write-off
Joseph remains scarless and intact.
Paula suffered one invisible blow
to the chest, from which she
will not recover.

In the Absence of Birds

Not even a crow, you mumble,
turning toward her as she raises the camera.
But there is still ground to cover:
cracking through the hoary undergrowth near
the stream bank, breaking a tire loose from the frozen earth
and dead leaves, *who rolled it this far from the road?*
The whole day's been an absentminded thought,
a collection of errors: losing the moon in the front closet
until the spring clean. Standing in the middle of a cold spell,
you can close your eyes and feel the water in them.

Something in the way of hollow bone has left you
unfamiliar, gone migrant then returned
from a long flight. A slow change
into what you have never wanted
but always loved as it escaped you.
It's the company you keep,
their steep demands on physics
and the inevitable.

This is the life someone else has chosen
and lived in lieu of me.

You carry this in your eyes as she takes the picture:
waiting for it to sink through the still air,
or grow wings and light in the trees behind you.
To bury you in the sky,
like the absence of birds that day;
the ones gathering in flocks under her heart.

Reading

Anxious fame. Already
I can tell you're a fan of Woody Allen,
as you heel-toe-shuffle onto the stage with a sheepish
imbalance, measuring the currents of smoke
and low drunken buzz, the floorboards' softness
for the least awkward face-plant. Imagining us nude
would not, I think, be helpful.

Under the hot lights the mic spits and crackles,
and a calculated pause fills your voice with
part honey, part rumba, and a trace of Denmark;
should've grown to love winter days.
We have been warned to hold our applause
for the end. Everyone but the bar staff
is listening.

Though light can open like hands and the full moon
does have several occupations, please,
do not refer to art. The "don't piss in my swimming pool I don't
swim in your toilet" rule applies here. Hackney and cliché
your way through the first few to calm the nerves,
lips whetted by each word. *Look what I did
to language. Again.* But save the best for last,
that impending, troubled punchline. An idea
that pivots unexpectedly, hovers
an instant in the thick air.

This is uncalled for.
I don't think I've ever wanted
to witness such a wounded,
unfamiliar heart laid bare.

Just make me laugh
between poems
and I'll forgive you.

Slow Cure

Walking in the park at twilight
sifting through the day, the heavy-bodied feeling
of anger at nothing, sharp silences and sex before dinner,
there are dishes need cleaning and who gets to do them,
these and other gestures. Touching your shoulder
when the news gets graphic; the small refuges
we live inside.

The wind comes up hard off the water
and with it the slow cure of the past,
a child's final thing: singing *The Lion
Sleeps Tonite* before bed, the laughter
and stories that turned death on its ear,
fearlessness, knowing your father loved your mother,
that his father did the same, the pleasure of remoteness
when the light went out—*sayonara, adios
campaneros*, good night, good night.

I do not remember, but one day
when that boy was playing alone with the lazy
intensity only children have, dipping
his lean, summery-brown arms into the frogless creek
behind the house, he stood to go home and, turning
on the moment, emptied himself into me like a cold glass of water.

Tonight the lake looks like a field of snow,
or the colour of wheat stubble under the moon.
My approach disturbs a treeful of sparrows,
sends them scrambling into the sky. Small, open hands
lifting innumerably and, all at once, away from here.

A Letter to Charlie Lukashevsky on His Birth

Dear Charlie, I write this from Mexico, a meagre greeting
from among the wandering dogs and horses asleep on the beach.
                                                    A desert
rife with the smell of spray-paint, manure, burning coal and
                                                    mesquite,
where life's business begins and ends each day unfinished,
                                                    abandoned
beside the Pacific. The dust here dries my throat. Clouds stretch
                                                    like young
animal bones across the sun. May these words, then, carry the cells
and atoms of Diego Rivera's homeland to you in their beleaguered
                                                    hands.

You'll read this much later, little man, but it's the idea of you now
that confounds. Beneath your ancient Buddha face, an elastic skull
in its tectonics, shifting slowly towards the human. Barely sensate,
untapped thought delayed in its pronunciation. You are a seam
                                                    in philosophy.
Undeniable. Unaware the future is vulnerable. I was sorry to hear
about the *bris*—I couldn't attend, but sympathized from a distance.
Any pain, I'm sure, has already been forgotten. That is an early
                                                    lesson.

There is nothing to fear in this world but a relentless lack of silence.
As soon as you are able, run from this. Do not fight cowards or
                                                    lovers
on the way, it does more harm than good. Never conceal your
                                                    intelligence,
which doesn't mean you should continually offer explanations.
It's been my experience only buffoons always have something to say.
Truth rarely occurs. When it does, it is often undervalued.
This holds no bearing on compassion.

Time becomes a slow revolt against the body—divert such black
moods by treating everything seriously, except yourself.
Afternoons spent at leisure are one of the greatest pleasures.
Enter them eagerly, and with ambition: create something
beautiful and meaningless. You will have returned
what has been given you. Forgive me, this has become
didactic, which I would also caution against.

One more thing. I remember being at a crowded party
your mother held years ago. She had just come outside with
                                                        candles
and I realized, amid the laughter and ferocious, drunken
conversation, she was the most powerful person on that porch.
I remember the light fluttering, moth-like, around each of us.
Like a moth, I remember the light that shone from her. And
                                                your father,
your father seems a gentle man. I do not know him well.

Fugue for the Gulf of Mexico

in three voices

because I am sad and old,
and I know the earth, and am sad.

—Pablo Neruda

Fugue for the Gulf of Mexico, as it sits on the page, should be viewed as a blue-print for performance rather than any final, authoritative structure. The piece has been scored for an alto, tenor, and bass performer, the alto being the first column, the tenor the second, and the bass being the third. While the columns and colours provide visual boundaries between voices, how they co-ordinate themselves is left open. For example, as the tenor passes from the subject to the countersubject and the answer in alto is introduced, the voices can either read contrapuntally or antiphonally from line to line. Contrapuntal sounding of voices results in the production of 'white noise', a seeming senselessness for those of us with less than acute aural attention. However, for all of its distortion, white noise drags musicality through it like a skeleton from a closet. This kind of performance is closer to a musical fugue in its atemporality, its overlap of sequence. An antiphonal line to line succession of voices blends the stanzas with greater clarity while emphasizing the ferrying motion between voices. That is, the voices reverberate at a slower tempo. Both techniques speak to different aspects of how the ear acquires music from noise. Even the extended solo episodes may contain, at the performers' discretion, echoes and resonances of sounds, words, and phrases from the other voices, in effect re-entering a contrapuntal conversation:

Shells, ears
chambered music
clambering up alongshore
as castaways, some deep-bowelled
recollection of sea-bottom
and threshold, the gulf's umbilici,
we name you
to own your song: bleeding tooth,
milky moon shell, flame helmet,
apple murex, wide-mouthed purpura,
lettered olive, true tulip, angel
wing, Noah's ark, lion's paw,
lightning venus, rosy fissurella,   wide mouthed purpura
cancelled limpet, wentletrap,   bleeding tooth
writhing shell, turkey wing, cat's eye, true tulip, angel
worm tube, flamingo tongue,   wing, Noah's ark,
                            tell me,   we name you to own
                                        your song
sea bottom's threshold,   tell me of the sea's capsized heart,
some deep-bowelled   a snail's foot, underwater dusk,
            castaways,   turbulent sutures between what
clambering up alongshore   I have forgotten.
chambered music,   Salt and calcareous
ears and shells.   solutions unmeditate me. Whorling
                 corpses on the beach bite my heels, then recede.

It should also be noted that while the bass pedal for the fugue makes its visual appearance only after the *stretto*, those three lines also serve as an *ostinato*, repeated at a level of near inaudibility by a 'fourth' performer, starting immediately after the introduction of the subject/countersubject and continuing throughout the rest of the piece. After the *stretto*, the bass performer joins the 'fourth' performer in one final, discernable repetition of the lines.

The gulf beats out
        intuitive time
cradling the day

a ponderous ark of
    creatures and habits
            rising up
like blood to the heart

*

My pulse   The gulf beats out
        a litany of   intuitive time
shells and seabirds   cradling the day

        sunken into   a ponderous ark of
the body, reaching from   creatures and habits
    each locked cell   rising up
toward a cancerous moon   like blood to the heart

*

        My pulse   The gulf beats out
                a litany of   intuitive time
        shells and seabirds   cradling the day

                sunken into   a ponderous ark of
        the body, reaching from   creatures and habits
            each locked cell   rising up
        toward a cancerous moon like blood to the heart

*

                My pulse
                        a litany of
                shells and seabirds

                        sunken into
                the body, reaching from
                    each locked cell
                toward a cancerous moon

shells, ears,

chambered music

Pull the funk from your voice and speak. What?
clambering up alongshore
You will never know how much my speechlessness
as castaways, some deep-bowelled
has to do with waiting for you to hear it.
recollection of sea-bottom

and threshold, the gulf's umbilici,

we name you
Pull the funk from your voice and speak. What?
to own your song: bleeding tooth,
You will never know how much my speechlessness
milky moon shell, flame helmet,
has to do with waiting for you to hear it.
apple murex, wide-mouthed purpura,

lettered olive, true tulip, angel

wing, Noah's ark, lion's paw,
Pull the funk from your voice and speak. What?
lightning venus, rosy fissurella,
You will never know how much my speechlessness
cancellated limpet, wentletrap,
has to do with waiting for you to hear it.
writhing shell, turkey wing, cat's eye,

worm tube, flamingo tongue,

          tell me,
Pull the funk from your voice and speak. What?
tell me of the sea's capsized heart,
You will never know how much my speechlessness
a snail's foot, underwater dusk,
has to do with waiting for you to hear it.
turbulent sutures between what

I have forgotten.

        Salt and calcareous
Pull the funk from your voice and speak. What?
solutions unmeditate me. Whorling
You will never know how much my speechlessness
corpses on the beach bite my heels, then recede.
has to do with waiting for you to hear it.

Bare-knuckled heat
    allows the mind
to scuttle crabwise

Pull the funk from your voice and speak. What?
You will never know how much my speechlessness
has to do with waiting for you to hear it.

in the panic grass
  on dunes, palm leaves
rasping the air when

Pull the funk from your voice and speak. What?
You will never know how much my speechlessness
has to do with waiting for you to hear it.

sobering stormclouds gather

*Pull *the funk from your voice and speak. What?*
You will never know how much my speechlessness

The waves surrender   Bare-knuckled heat
   needlessness   allows the mind
the forgotten urge   to scuttle crabwise

Pull the funk from your voice and speak. What?

swelling up dumbly   in the panic grass
  in my mouth   on dunes, palm leaves
  driving through   rasping the air when

from water's dry interior   sobering stormclouds gather

You will never know how much my speechlessness
has to do with waiting for you to hear it.   *

                   The waves surrender

Pull the funk from your voice and speak.   needlessness
You will never know how much my the forgotten urge
has to do with waiting for you to hear it.

                   swelling up dumbly
                      in my mouth
Pull the funk from your voice and speak driving through
You will never know how much my speechlessness
has to do with waiting for you to from water's dry interior

first, winds punch
the thin treeline,
a sudden darkening,
then lightning over water,
water and light driven into water,
the gulf's articulation blurs
to a burr in a cloud's throat,
a dimpled pearl withdrawing
to the inner recess
where fish rest motionless.

What do I mean to speak of this
muted core, an indistinct threat
sheltered under the loosening
structure of unsalvaged wrecks?

The waves move seriously
bracing the storm's affair,
a shy lover refusing to become
                              unhinged completely;
the seabed, silent, lies
somewhere between familiarity
and desire.

I want to release an idea, gauge
the many entrances to water
but a sense of concealment
leaves me helpless, rendered in sand, dissolving
on the gulf's blistered margins.

94

Pull the funk from your voice and speak. What?
You will never know how much my speechlessness
has to do with waiting for you to hear it.

On invisible vectors
a tern
plunge-dives below

the surface and
the moment collapses
the mirror of

this grey impacted sky

Pull the funk from your voice and speak. What?
You will never know how much my speechlessness
has to do with waiting for you to hear it.

On invisible vectors
a tern
plunge-dives below
the surface and
the moment collapses
the mirror of
this grey impacted sky

My lungs clench
in the salt water
suddenly remembering

the long crawl
up for air
that first gasp
a toothache for memory

*

My lungs clench
in the salt water
suddenly remembering

the long crawl
up for air
that first gasp
a toothache for memory

Pull the funk from your voice and speak. What?
You will never know what this namelessness
has to do with waiting

seabirds
distant, twigging on
imperceptible wind-lags
like kites, or landing
with bulk and steady ease,
the functioning grace
in the ponderous, combustion
held together by wind, torque
flight-feather and patience,
         a coiled inertia reel, eye combing the surf
the thirty foot drop impacting
on one more meal, we name you
to hollow our bones for flight:
brown pelican, magnificent frigate
aka man-o'-war aka hurricane bird,
pectoral piper, royal tern, willet,
great blue heron, double-crested
cormorant, reddish egret, long-billed
curlew, tropicbird, sanderling,
ruddy turnstone, laughing gull,
                    show me,
show me a fish trail,
the acumen of seeing through water,
the necessity of routine, how to
wait rather than remember. The chorus
of gulls and terns clotting on the shore
drowns me out. Sandpipers don't give
second glances as they escort the advancing tide

Five dolphin backs
  brief and dense
  curl over like

cogs turning
  on tidal gears
a subtle timepiece
resolving the day's tempo

My eyes against
  a vague horizon
sand-scored fossils

  the mechanism of
a blind man waking
  to move into

another stage of dreams

Five dolphin backs
brief and dense
curl over like

cogs turning
on tidal gears
a subtle timepiece

resolving the day's tempo

My eyes against
a vague horizon
sand-scored fossils

the mechanism of
a blind man waking
to move into

another stage of dreams

Pull the funk from your voice and speak. What?
You will never know how much my speechlessness
has to do with waiting for you to hear it.

97

the gulf is a pulse
a blind tempo
driven through tons
of water to quicken
and slim time   this time, this time

       remembers
       too much,
       says even more speaking for
                 what the gulf
                 has not told
                 leaves me stranded
       we are stranded
       oceans
       beneath skin
       still drawn
chancred moon   by the moon
tropical eye
shuffling tides
and the habits
of my blood   the blood rushes
            to the heart's
            trapped center
            as I float belly-up
            eyes filled
            with salt water   through sea water
                               a shell hears
                               each day's rumours
                               turn over
            the tides may   in the tides
            rise and flood
            my lungs once more
       so my tongue becomes
       a furled wing, a silent pelican,
       having learned to watch for storm fronts.

Pull the funk from your voice and speak. What?
You will never know how much my speechlessness
has to do with waiting for you to hear it.

The gulf beats out
        intuitive time
cradling the day

a ponderous ark of
    creatures and habits
          rising up
like blood to the heart

Notes

Kyōka
The Japanese poetic term translates as "mad waka", or "mad verse", and was, in its time, characterized by a jocular "lowness" linguistically, often challenging the authority of established poets (Bashō and Buson being no exception) in order to appeal to popular audiences. Kyōka were composed as early as the Kamakura Period, but at the time waka was such an esteemed form the kyōka's parody and language play could not be officially acknowledged as a legitimate art. The form reached its height in the Muromachi and Edo Periods. During these periods haikai was gaining dominance and kyōka appeared chiefly as irrational, playful haiku. Examples of formally astute Kyōka can be found in the work of Ishida Mitoku, Shoku Sanjin, Matsunaga Teitoku, Ota Nampō, and Seihakudo Gyōfū (a student of Teitoku's). I have informally taken the term kyōka to mean *haiku-gone-awry*—thought about phenomena, the language of such thought, spinning off its axes.

Head Arrangements: Twelve-String Poems for Huddie Ledbetter
The tagline, or end line, of each poem is a lyric from one of Leadbelly's songs (in order of poems): "Green Corn", "Good Morning Blues", "Looky Looky Yonder, Where the Sun Done Gone", "Matchbox Blues", "When I Was a Cowboy", "John Hardy", "Where Did You Sleep Last Night", "Midnight Special", "Yellow Woman's Doorbells", "Daddy I'm Coming Back to You", "We're in the Same Boat, Brother", "Grey Goose".

A Letter to Charlie Lukashevsky On His Birth
Charlie Lukashevsky (2002-   ) is the son of Liza Ormsby and Alex Lukashevsky. Diego Rivera (1886-1957) was a Mexican artist in the 20's and 30's whose oversized murals, often politically interpreted, revived the fresco style in both Mexico and the United States.

A *bris or brith*, derived from the Hebrew *berith*, is the Judaic ritual surrounding circumcision, usually performed eight days after birth.

Head Arrangements is for Adrienne Barnett.

Reading is for Karen Solie.

In the Absence of Birds is for Don McKay, and for Jan Zwicky who took the picture.

Epigraph sources:

Epigraph by Martin Heidegger from "The Origin of the Work of Art" in *Poetry, Language, Thought* translated by Albert Hofstadter.

Epigraph by Walter Benjamin from *Schriften, Vol.1* as translated by Harry Zohn in Hannah Arendt's introduction to *Illuminations*.

Epigraph by Don McKay from the poem "Alluvium" as it appears in his chapbook *Varves*.

Epigraph by Gilles Deleuze from the appendix to *Logic of Sense* translated by Mark Lester with Charles Stivale.

Epigraph by Paul Celan from the poem "Argumentum e Silentio" translated by Michael Hamburger.

Epigraph by Tomas Tranströmer from the poem "Streets in Shanghai" translated by Samuel Charters.

Epigraph by Pablo Neruda from the poem "Melancholy in the Families" translated by Donald Walsh.

Errata
Where you see *light*, read *emptiness*. Substitute the word *beautiful* with *difficult*.
Remove all references to the *heart* and do not replace.

Acknowledgements

Earlier versions of some of these poems have appeared in *The Malahat Review, Prism international, Arc, Prairie Fire, The Fiddlehead,* and *Breathing Fire 2: Canada's New Poets* (Nightwood Editions, 2004). *Head Arrangements: Twelve-String Poems for Huddie Ledbetter* was published as a chapbook by Junction Books in February 2004. Much appreciation to the respective editors. The author also gratefully acknowledges the support of the Canada Council for the Arts.

For unswerving editorial advice on these poems, and for constant support and friendship in this endeavour, and more, my thanks to Adrienne Barrett, Steve McOrmond, Matthew Tierney. It all lasts.

My deepest gratitude to Don McKay and Jan Zwicky for their encouragement over the years. Don's unerring insights and sculptor's touch in the shaping of this manuscript have been crucial. I remain indebted to Jan for the exacting, philosophically attuned ear with which she undertook the editing of this final incarnation. Jan, Don, what more. I cannot ask.

To my others: Christopher, through hell and high water. To Morgan Wade and Mark Uygur, to Chris Evans, Darryl Gould, Janet Hoops, Ken Howe, Zameret Kleiman, Izabella Klüft, Alayna Munce, Charmaine Tierney, Silas White, Carleton Wilson, and to those who nurtured these poems through their formative stages: Adam Dickinson, Shane Rhodes, Sue Sinclair, Murray Sutcliffe, Andy Weaver, the participants and conveners of the 1998 writing colloquium at St. Peter's Abbey in Muenster, Saskatchewan, the participants and faculty of the Banff Centre for the Arts 2003 Writing Studio. And to Russell Crowe, for his inadvertent patronage.

To my brother Jeff and sister Rhea, and my parents, you are all here in this.

And Nora, a chuck on the chin for your staggering, synaptic ease with language, with me, for incisive moments as silent as, for motel lams, for your headlong leaps into the more dangerous cases, for the now and the much laters. I'll meet you at the Klondike, darling. You are intrepid, and swell. You're the cat's meow.

David Seymour was born in Campbellton, New Brunswick and was raised beside the Niagara Escarpment in Milton, Ontario. In the past ten years he has lived in Hamilton, Ontario, Leith, Scotland, Fredericton, New Brunswick, Toronto, Ontario, and Rosarito Beach, Mexico. During that time he has worked as a security guard, built pools, dish-pigged, acquired two academic degrees, lectured, led university tutorials, worked as a video store clerk, a bookstore clerk, proofread, been editorial coordinator for a magazine company, freelance wrote, played an extra, photo-doubled for Russell Crowe, been an off-camera reader, learned sailing skills on a tall ship, and worked as the production assistant for a casting director on several films. He currently lives in Toronto.